YOUNG ABE LINCOLN

◄── The Frontier Days, 1809-1837 ──►

Written and illustrated by Cheryl Harness

NATIONAL
GEOGRAPHIC
SOCIETY

Washington, D.C.

February 12, 1809

Winter winds were whooping and whipping round the cabin in the Kentucky woods. They cried at the chinks in the stout log walls, but they couldn't get inside the firelit cabin where a new boy baby lay safe and warm in his mother's arms.

Tom Lincoln smiled at two-year-old Sarah: "Look now, here's your brother, Abraham. He'll soon be a'taggin' along after you, shirttail a'flappin'."

Six winters later, Nancy Lincoln was sewing buckskin breeches for her little boy to wear to school in the spring, once the crops were planted. A proud smile lighted her thin face. She said, "It's a precious thing to larn readin', writin' and cipherin'. You and your sister have a chance I never got."

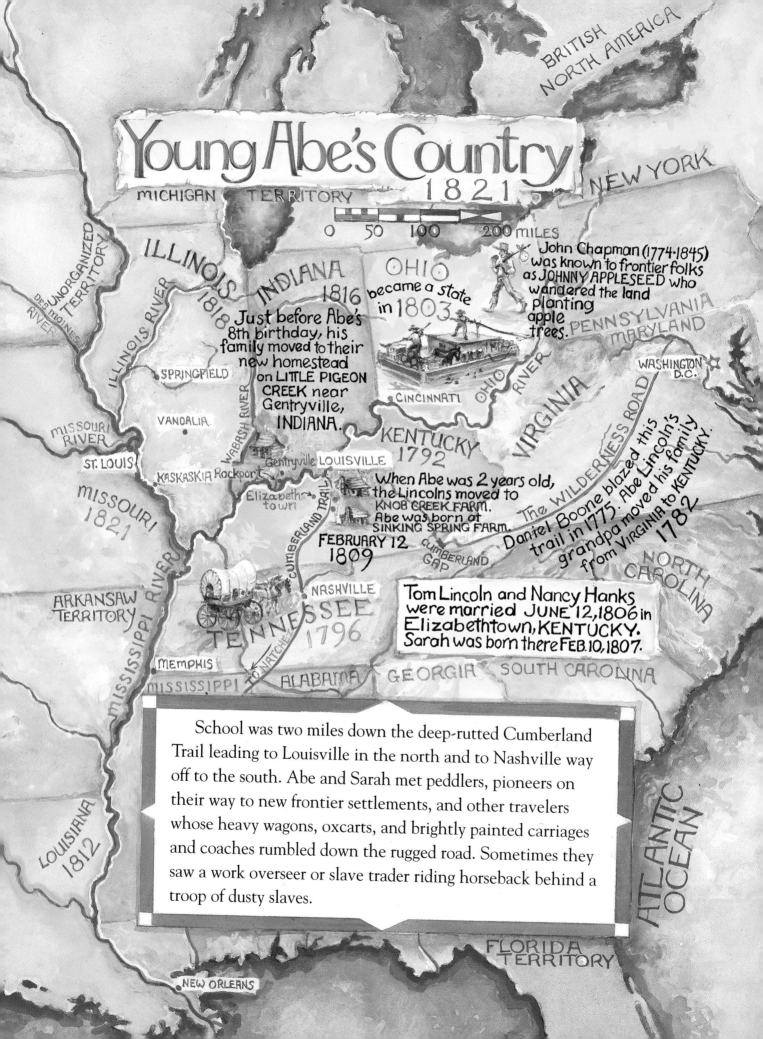

Young Abe's Country
1821

MICHIGAN TERRITORY

BRITISH NORTH AMERICA

NEW YORK

0   50   100   200 MILES

ILLINOIS 1818

UNORGANIZED TERRITORY

DES MOINES RIVER

ILLINOIS RIVER

SPRINGFIELD

VANDALIA

MISSOURI RIVER

ST. LOUIS

KASKASKIA

MISSOURI 1821

MISSISSIPPI RIVER

ARKANSAW TERRITORY

LOUISIANA 1812

NEW ORLEANS

INDIANA 1816

Just before Abe's 8th birthday, his family moved to their new homestead on LITTLE PIGEON CREEK near Gentryville, INDIANA.

WABASH RIVER

Gentryville

Rockport

Elizabethtown

OHIO became a state in 1803

CINCINNATI

OHIO RIVER

John Chapman (1774·1845) was known to frontier folks as JOHNNY APPLESEED who wandered the land planting apple trees.

PENNSYLVANIA

MARYLAND

WASHINGTON D.C.

VIRGINIA

KENTUCKY 1792

LOUISVILLE

When Abe was 2 years old, the Lincolns moved to KNOB CREEK FARM. Abe was born at SINKING SPRING FARM.

FEBRUARY 12 1809

CUMBERLAND TRAIL

CUMBERLAND GAP

The WILDERNESS ROAD Daniel Boone blazed this trail in 1775. Abe Lincoln's grandpa moved his family from VIRGINIA to KENTUCKY 1782

NORTH CAROLINA

NASHVILLE

TENNESSEE 1796

Tom Lincoln and Nancy Hanks were married JUNE 12, 1806 in Elizabethtown, KENTUCKY. Sarah was born there FEB.10, 1807.

MEMPHIS

NATCHEZ TRACE

MISSISSIPPI   ALABAMA   GEORGIA   SOUTH CAROLINA

FLORIDA TERRITORY

ATLANTIC OCEAN

School was two miles down the deep-rutted Cumberland Trail leading to Louisville in the north and to Nashville way off to the south. Abe and Sarah met peddlers, pioneers on their way to new frontier settlements, and other travelers whose heavy wagons, oxcarts, and brightly painted carriages and coaches rumbled down the rugged road. Sometimes they saw a work overseer or slave trader riding horseback behind a troop of dusty slaves.

When Abe and Sarah got to the tiny school cabin, they heard
a sing-songy gabble.

"Don't be skairt, Abey," said Sarah. "It's jes the way they read their lessons,
out loud like that so's the master kin tell they're studyin'."

Tall Mr. Riney set them to reciting and learning letters and numbers.
When school ended at harvest time, Abe had learned to write words. He liked
making words on a board with a piece of charcoal, on a shovel with a bit of
soapstone, or in the dust with a stick.

"ABE!" His father's voice came hollering from the fields, breaking into Abe's
daydreams. "Come git to work!"

Way off to the north of their farm, just beyond the Ohio River, was Indiana. Partly because Tom Lincoln didn't approve of slavery, which was legal in Kentucky, he moved his family to Indiana. Abe's gray eyes were wide with astonishment when he saw the mighty river and imagined the cold waters down and dark beneath the raft.

That icy December of 1816, Indiana became the 19th state in the Union. The Lincolns quickly built a three-sided shelter on their homestead near Little Pigeon Creek. On the fourth side was a blazing, smoking fire that could never be allowed to go out. It saved them from freezing to death and scared the wolves and panthers away.

Before spring came to the Indiana woods, neighbors were
stomping and whistling through the snowy forest to help the
newcomers build a cabin, as was the frontier custom. Seven-year-old
Abe swung his ax alongside the big boys and whiskery men.

Hunting and gathering food, clearing the land, splitting log rails for fences, and hauling water left no time for school. Besides, there wasn't any school to go to. Abe practiced writing and listened hard when grown-ups were talking. He wanted to remember and understand words and ideas.

Abe was glad when his mother's relatives, Tom and Betsy Sparrow and 17-year-old Dennis Hanks, came from Kentucky to live nearby.

"It's so good to see homefolks!" Nancy cried. She was worn thin with work and lonely for news from home.

Barely a year later, when farmers were getting in the harvest of 1818, fearsome word went traveling through the forest: The "milk sickness" was killing cows and people. By the 5th of October, the Sparrows had died and Nancy followed after.

Tom and Dennis sawed the boards, Abe whittled the pine pegs, then Sarah lined the narrow coffin with Nancy's best quilt.

Nine-year-old Abe was sunk in sadness, too sad for words. Too sad. It was the loneliest time.

Eleven-year-old Sarah tried to make corn dodgers and stew as good as Nancy's, tried to keep the dirt-floored cabin clean and their clothes washed and mended. Tom, Abe, and Dennis, wearing "boots" made of tree bark, worked outside from dawn to dark. They could hear the ringing of other men's axes way off all through the woods along Little Pigeon Creek.

One night at supper Tom said, "We're gonna have us a church and a school. We got enough folks hereabouts to pay a teacher now."

Abe felt like he was being wakened from a long, gloomy dream. "School?"

Cousin Dennis puffed a smoke ring from his cob pipe and Tom smiled. "Yep, there's gonna be a school startin' after harvest. Your ma had her...um...a hunger for larnin' for you young'uns. She'll have been gone a long hard year, come fall and—"

Tom cleared his throat noisily and said, "I'll be off then to Kentuck' fer a spell. Got me some business to tend to."

Abe and his sister walked a mile and a half to the school cabin, shook hands with Mr. Crawford, the schoolmaster, and took their places at the split-log desks and benches. They and the other children studied such books as Webster's *Blue-backed Speller* and Murray's *English Reader*.

They hurried home in the cold gray afternoons. Chores were waiting. "Spellin' and readin' beats cookin' and carryin' water ANY day!" Sarah exclaimed.

Abe swept off his coonskin cap and recited grandly:

"Good boys who to their books apply

Will be great men by and by."

Sarah pushed him off his stump with a playful shove.

Just in sight of the cabin one December afternoon, Abe and Sarah heard heavy wheels and the plodding of heavy horses coming through the woods. High on the buckboard of a huge wagon sat Tom Lincoln and a rosy-faced woman. Abe stood at the edge of the clearing, shivering in his tattered buckskins. Sarah pulled her mother's old shawl close about her shoulders. They stared.

Tom helped the lady down, saying as he did so, "Here's your new ma, Sally Bush Johnston. I knowed her when I was a boy and she a little gal. Her husband's done passed away and these'uns are her girls, Sarah Elizabeth and Matilda, and her boy, John." Three long-legged children climbed down off the featherbed on top of the load of bundles and furniture. "We'll be a family together," Tom finished in a rush.

The new Mrs. Lincoln patted Sarah's cheek. "My Elizabeth has a dress just your size, I reckon. Then we'll do us some sewing." Turning to Abe, she said, "I hear you're a scholar. How old are you, Abraham?"

"Yes, ma'am," Abe whispered. "Eleven, this coming February, ma'am."

"There're books in my trunk, Abraham," she said kindly, pushing Abe's rough dark hair back out of his eyes. "We'll get along fine." She bowed her bonnet to Dennis Hanks, who was standing with his mouth open in the cabin doorway.

Sally gave the cabin a sharp look.

"Tom! Fetch me some water! We got to be scrubbin' before there's any unpackin'!"

Abe's pants were always too short, seemed like, as he grew tall and taller working in his father's fields, reading Sally's books. He memorized *Aesop's Fables*, read over and over her *Robinson Crusoe* and *Pilgrim's Progress* and her Bible. Abe walked for miles to borrow the few books owned by his frontier neighbors. He listened to the rivermen and farmers talking politics in Mr. Gentry's store.

As the Lincoln farm was more prosperous, Abe wore rawhide boots on his big feet. He grew strong swinging his ax and wrenching out tree stumps, but he preferred reading the law books in Judge Pete's and Lawyer Pitcher's offices and reciting the political speeches he'd memorized from the newspapers.

"That boy's always got his lazy nose in a book," Tom muttered. "He's had all the larnin' a man needs, ain't he?"

"He's got a head full of questions," Sally said fondly.

Just before Abe's 19th birthday in 1828, Abe's sister Sarah, who had been Mrs. Aaron Grigsby since the summer of 1826, died along with her baby in childbirth. After this tragedy, Abe grew even more thoughtful. He missed her.

When Abe "hired out" to do farm work or cut wood for others, and when he began working on the Ohio as a boatman, Abe turned his wages over to his father. This was the proper custom until Abe was 21, when he "came of age."

One afternoon, Mr. Gentry told Abe, "I've a load of goods to be sold in New Orleans and I need a flatboatman. You interested? I'll pay $8.00 a month and your steamboat ticket home."

Abe and Mr. Gentry's son, Allen, built the flatboat 18 feet wide and 65 feet long, loaded the cargo, and pushed off for a voyage of a thousand miles down the Ohio and Mississippi Rivers. It took skill to read the rivers' currents and strength to pilot the big boat around the bends, through storms, past log rafts, barges, and steamboats.

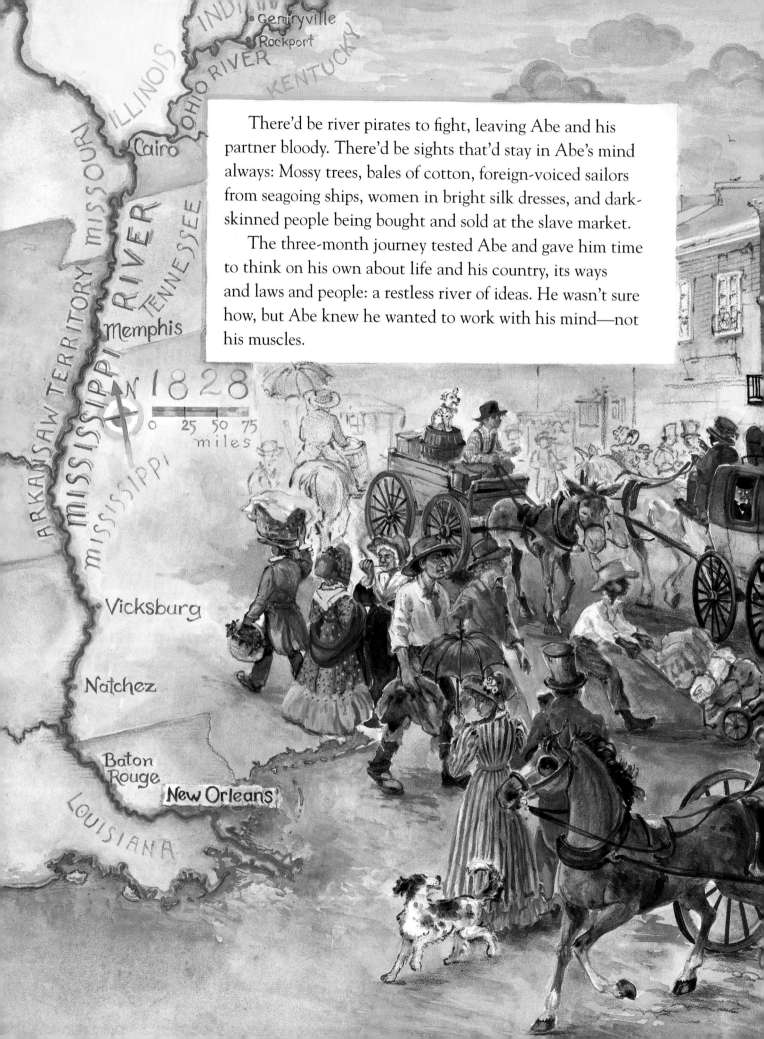

There'd be river pirates to fight, leaving Abe and his partner bloody. There'd be sights that'd stay in Abe's mind always: Mossy trees, bales of cotton, foreign-voiced sailors from seagoing ships, women in bright silk dresses, and dark-skinned people being bought and sold at the slave market.

The three-month journey tested Abe and gave him time to think on his own about life and his country, its ways and laws and people: a restless river of ideas. He wasn't sure how, but Abe knew he wanted to work with his mind—not his muscles.

In his own way, Tom was restless, too. He'd heard of good land out west in Illinois. Tom and Sally, her grown children and their families, and Dennis Hanks, who'd married one of Sally's daughters, all moved to Illinois just after Abe's 21st birthday in 1830.

As he didn't have a clear idea of just what he wanted to do, Abe went along too.

After one of the coldest of Illinois winters, Abe finally said good-bye to his family. As he described himself later on, Abe was a floating piece of driftwood who came to a stop in the tiny village of New Salem, Illinois, on the Sangamon River, July 1831.

ABE LINCOLN became a soldier in the BLACK HAWK WAR of 1832 when the old SAUK Chief fought a losing battle to reclaim his tribal lands in northern ILLINOIS. ABE'S fellow soldiers elected him captain.

The LINCOLN clan homesteaded on the north bank of the SANGAMON RIVER ten miles west of DECATUR. A year later they moved on 100 miles southeast.

ABE left behind his father, his stepmother, Sarah, her three grown children and their families including Abe's cousin Dennis Hanks who had married Mrs. LINCOLN's daughter, Sarah Elizabeth.

By the time he left New Salem six years later, Abe had earned a reputation as an able boatman, honest postmaster, storekeeper, land surveyor, soldier, and a wrestler who could throw the toughest guys around, then shake hands and tell a funny story.

He studied with the schoolmaster and borrowed law books from Lawyer Stuart 16 miles away over in the town of Springfield.

Abe studied grammar and joined the New Salem Debating Society to learn to speak his ideas with force and logic. He had decided to be a politician and represent his neighbors at the Illinois General Assembly in Vandalia. People laughed at how he looked, then liked how he talked. Abe got elected on his second try in 1834. He was 25 years old.

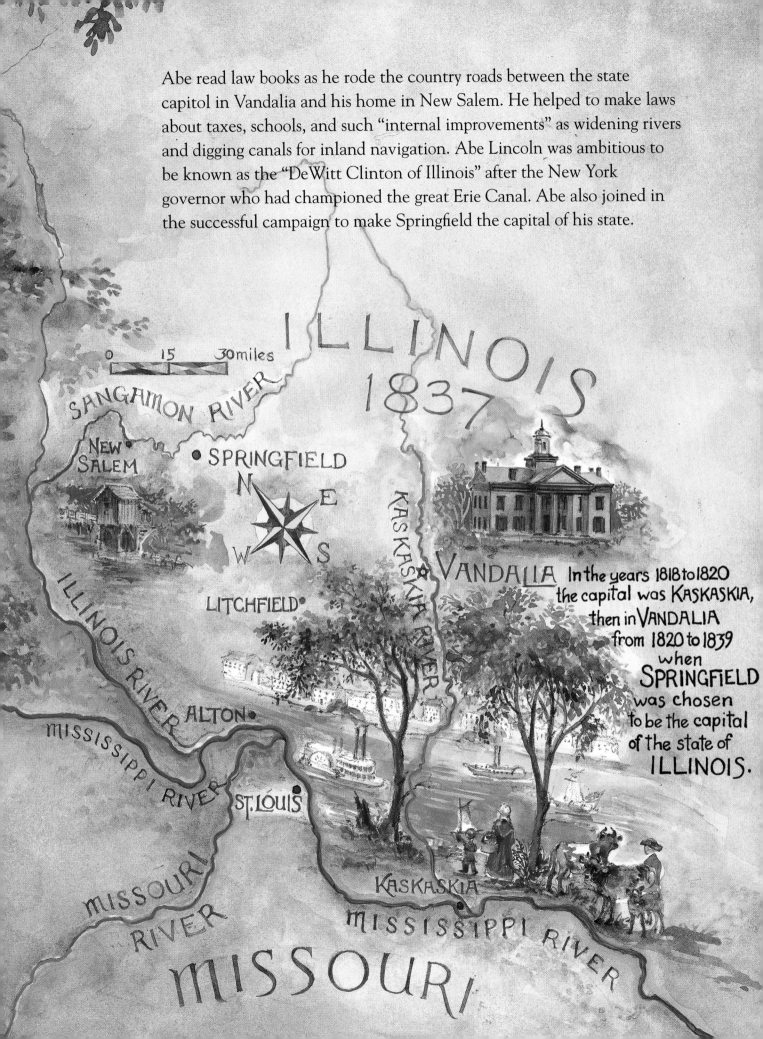

Abe read law books as he rode the country roads between the state capitol in Vandalia and his home in New Salem. He helped to make laws about taxes, schools, and such "internal improvements" as widening rivers and digging canals for inland navigation. Abe Lincoln was ambitious to be known as the "DeWitt Clinton of Illinois" after the New York governor who had championed the great Erie Canal. Abe also joined in the successful campaign to make Springfield the capital of his state.

ILLINOIS 1837

0 15 30 miles

SANGAMON RIVER

NEW SALEM

SPRINGFIELD

N E W S

LITCHFIELD

KASKASKIA RIVER

VANDALIA

In the years 1818 to 1820 the capital was KASKASKIA, then in VANDALIA from 1820 to 1839 when SPRINGFIELD was chosen to be the capital of the state of ILLINOIS.

ILLINOIS RIVER

MISSISSIPPI RIVER

ALTON

ST. LOUIS

MISSOURI RIVER

KASKASKIA

MISSISSIPPI RIVER

MISSOURI

When Abe was 28 years old, he packed his saddlebags with his clothes and books. He tucked his new license to practice law in the band of his silk stovepipe hat and trotted out of New Salem with a wave goodbye to his neighbors.

"So long, Abe," his friends called after him.